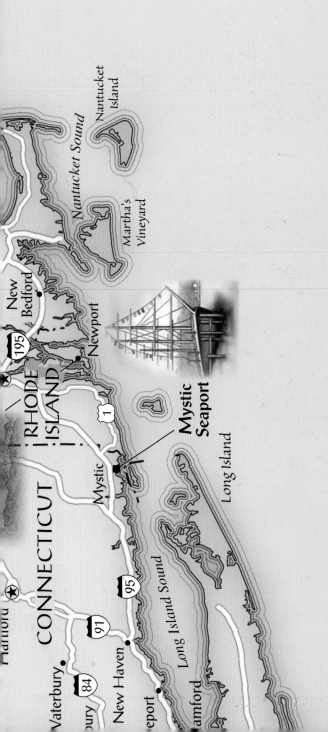

Nantucket Island

Nantucket Sound

Martha's Vineyard

New Bedford

195

Newport

RHODE ISLAND

**Mystic Seaport**

1

Mystic

Long Island

Long Island Sound

CONNECTICUT

Hartford

Waterbury

84

91

New Haven

95

eport

amford

Long Island

# CAROL M. HIGHSMITH AND TED LANDPHAIR

# NEW ENGLAND COAST

## A PHOTOGRAPHIC TOUR

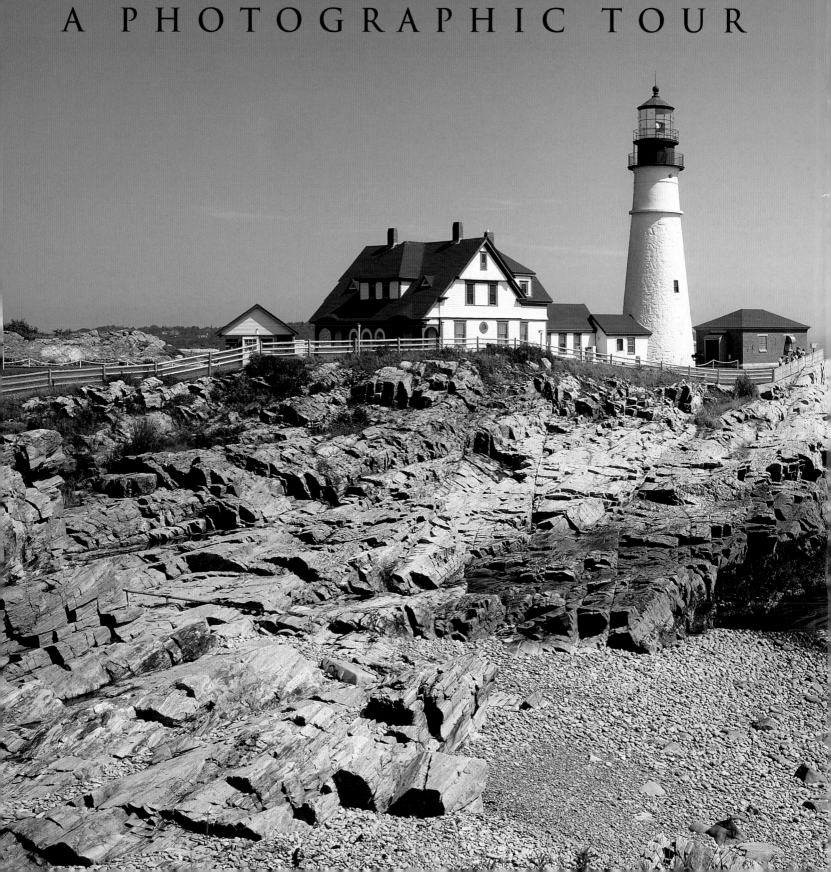

CRESCENT BOOKS

NEW YORK

FRONT COVER: On a Bailey's Island cove in Maine, Eddie and Doris Evans own a typical, oft-sketched fish house, built before 1900. Here, sea salts built lobster traps and tarred nets. BACK COVER: Lower Cape Cod's quaint harbors include Wellfleet, only two miles wide but stretching seventy-five miles into the Atlantic. The town has become a prominent art center. Its wildlife sanctuary offers captivating nature walks. Cape Cod National Seashore covers the entire ocean side of town. PAGE 1: Drivers must watch for children, deer, and moose elsewhere in New England, but on the coast, they look for crossing crustaceans! PAGES 2–3: Portland Head Light at Fort Williams is one of the most popular attractions in Maine's largest city.

Photographs copyright © 1999
by Carol M. Highsmith
Text copyright © 1999
by Random House Value Publishing, Inc.
All rights reserved under International and
Pan-American Copyright Conventions.

This 1999 edition is published by Crescent Books®,
an imprint of
Random House Value Publishing, Inc.,
201 East 50th Street, New York, N.Y. 10022.

Crescent Books® and colophon
are registered trademarks of
Random House Value Publishing, Inc.

Random House
New York • Toronto • London • Sydney • Auckland
http://www.randomhouse.com/

Printed and bound in China

Library of Congress Cataloging-in-Publication Data

Highsmith, Carol M.
New England Coast /
Carol M. Highsmith and Ted Landphair.
p.   cm. — (A photographic tour)
Includes index.
ISBN 0-517-20404-5 (hc: alk. paper)
1. Atlantic Coast (New England)—Tours.
2. Atlantic Coast (New England)—Pictorial works.
I. Landphair, Ted, 1942–   . II. Title. III. Series:
Highsmith, Carol M., 1946–   Photographic tour.
F12.A74H54  1999                    98–35689
917.404´43—dc21                      CIP

8  7  6  5  4  3  2

Project Editor: Donna Lee Lurker
Production Supervisor: Milton Wackerow
Designed by Robert L. Wiser, Archetype Press, Inc.,
Washington, D.C.

All photographs by Carol M. Highsmith unless otherwise credited: map by XNR Productions, page 5; painting by Kate Huntington, Providence, Rhode Island, page 6; Barnum Museum, Bridgeport, Connecticut, page 8; Old Lighthouse Museum and Historical Society, Stonington, Connecticut, page 9; Newport, Rhode Island, Historical Society, page 10; Plimoth Plantation, Plymouth, Massachusetts, page 11; John F. Kennedy Museum, Hyannis, Cape Cod, page 12; Cape Cod Pilgrim Memorial Association, page 13; Harbor Realty and Property Management, Salem, Massachusetts, page 15; Strawbery Banke Museum, Portsmouth, New Hampshire, page 14; Samoset Resort, Rockport, Maine, page 16; Maine Maritime Museum, Bath, Maine, pages 17, 18, 19, 21; Franklin D. Roosevelt Library, Hyde Park, New York, page 20.

THE AUTHORS WISH TO THANK THE FOLLOWING FOR THEIR GENEROUS ASSISTANCE AND HOSPITALITY IN CONNECTION WITH THE COMPLETION OF THIS BOOK

DESTINNATIONS NEW ENGLAND
RESERVATIONS AND ITINERARIES
West Yarmouth, Massachusetts

NANCY MARSHALL COMMUNICATIONS
on behalf of
MAINE OFFICE OF TOURISM

Jerry and Arden Brady, Annapolis, Maryland

CONNECTICUT

Amarante's Custom Catering, New Haven; Lynne Liscek Black, Coastal Fairfield County Convention and Visitor Bureau; Neil Sheridan and Jack Karle, East Haddam; Reneson Loisel, Greater New Haven Convention & Visitors Bureau; Margaret York, Greenwich

MAINE

Balance Rock Inn, Bar Harbor, Nancy Cloud, Innkeeper; Captain Daniel Stone Inn, Brunswick, Louisa C. Holmes, Innkeeper; Harbor House on Sawyer Cove, Jonesport, Maureen and Gene Hart, Innkeepers; Inn by the Sea, Cape Elizabeth, Maureen L. McQuade, Owner/Innkeeper; Newagen Seaside Inn, Southport Island, Heidi Larsen, Innkeeper; Old Fort Inn, Kennebunkport, David Aldrich, Innkeeper; Samoset Resort, Rockport, Jim Ash, General Manager; Snow Squall Bed & Breakfast Inn, Wiscasset, Anne and Steve Kornacki, Innkeepers; Weston House Bed and Breakfast Inn, Eastport, Jett and John Peterson, Innkeepers; Woods Hole, Martha's Vineyard & Nantucket Steamship Authority, Debbie Hughes, Marketing Director; Peter Dow Bachelder, Ellsworth; Dale Fardelman Harbor Tours, Jonesport; Charlotte Johnson, Nancy Marshall Communications

MASSACHUSETTS

Belfry Inne and Bistro, Sandwich, Chris Wilson, Innkeeper; Blueberry Manor, Yarmouthport, Cape Cod, Gerald Rosen and Victoria Schul, Innkeepers; Colonial Inn, Edgartown, Martha's Vineyard, Linda Malcouronne, General Manager; Harbor Light Inn, Marblehead, Peter Conway, Proprietor; Ralph Waldo Emerson Inn, Pigeon Cove, Rockport, Bruce Coats, General Manager; Woods Hole, Martha's Vineyard & Nantucket Steamship Authority, Debbie Hughes, Marketing Director; Peggie Hunter, Destinnations New England; Tracy M. O'Reilly, Nantucket Island Chamber of Commerce

NEW HAMPSHIRE

Mount Washington Hotel and Resort, Bretton Woods, Cathy Bedor, Director of Marketing; Sise Inn, Portsmouth, Lorie Kurtz, Innkeeper

RHODE ISLAND

Indian Beacon Inn, South Kingstown, Sarah and Robert Ryan, Proprietors; Spring House Hotel, Old Harbor, Block Island; Cindy Kelly, Mixed Media Gallery, Old Harbor, Block Island; Ann O'Neill, South County Tourism Council; Nina Stack, Block Island Tourism Council

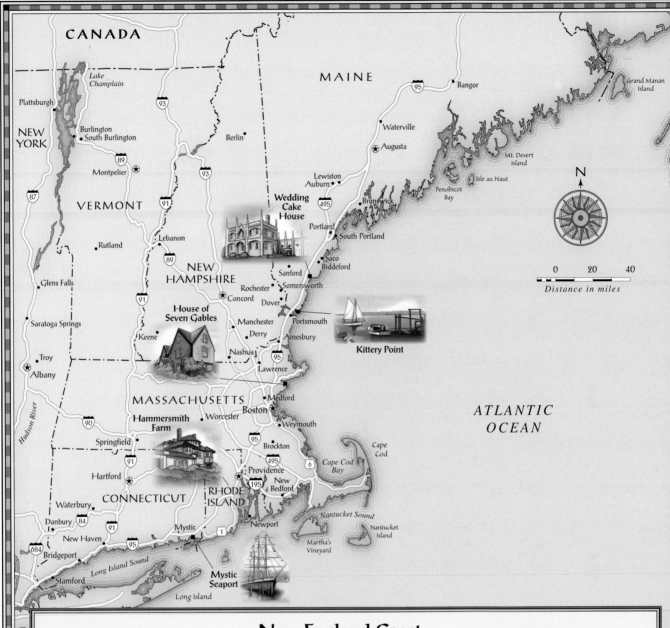

CANADA

MAINE

NEW YORK

Plattsburgh

Lake Champlain

Burlington
South Burlington

Berlin

Bangor

Waterville

Augusta

Montpelier

VERMONT

Lewiston
Auburn

Brunswick

Mt. Desert Island

Grand Manan Island

Isle au Haut

Penobscot Bay

Rutland

Lebanon

Portland
South Portland

**Wedding Cake House**

Saco
Biddeford

NEW HAMPSHIRE

Sanford

Glens Falls

Rochester
Concord

Somersworth

Dover

**House of Seven Gables**

Saratoga Springs

Keene

Manchester

Portsmouth

N

Troy
Albany

Derry

Amesbury

Nashua

Lawrence

**Kittery Point**

0   20   40

*Distance in miles*

ATLANTIC OCEAN

MASSACHUSETTS

Medford

**Hammersmith Farm**

Worcester

Boston

Weymouth

Hudson River

Springfield

Brockton

Cape Cod

Hartford

Providence

New Bedford

Cape Cod Bay

Waterbury

RHODE ISLAND

CONNECTICUT

Danbury

New Haven

Mystic

Newport

Nantucket Sound

Nantucket Island

Martha's Vineyard

Bridgeport

**Mystic Seaport**

Stamford

Long Island Sound

Long Island

# New England Coast

**Connecticut**
Capital: Hartford
Statehood: January 9, 1788 (5th state)
Area: 4,845 square miles (12,550 sq km)
Origin of name: *Quinnehtukqut,* Indian word meaning "beside the long tidal river"
Nickname: The Nutmeg State
State animal: Sperm whale
State bird: American robin
State flower: Mountain laurel
State tree: White oak
State ship: *USS Nautilus*
State song: "Yankee Doodle"
State motto: *Qui transtulit sustinet* ("He who transplanted still sustains)
Average January temperature: 25°F (-4°C)
Average July temperature: 73°F (23°C)

**Rhode Island**
Capital: Providence
Statehood: May 29, 1790 (13th state)
Area: 1,045 square miles (2,706 sq km)
Origin of name: From the Greek island of Rhodes
Nickname: The Ocean State

State bird: Rhode Island red
State flower: Violet
State tree: Red maple
State song: "Rhode Island"
State motto: "Hope"
Average January temperature: 28°F (-2°C)
Average July temperature: 72°F (23°C)

**Massachusetts**
Capital: Boston
Statehood: February 6, 1788 (6th state)
Area: 7,838 square miles (20,300 sq km)
Origin of name: Indian word meaning "green mountain place"
Nicknames: Bay State, Old Colony State
State bird: Chickadee
State flower: Mayflower
State tree: American elm
State song: "All Hail to Massachusetts"
State motto: *Ense petit placidam sub libertate quietem* ("By the sword we seek peace, but peace only under liberty")
Average January temperature: 30°F (-1°C)
Average July temperature: 74°F (23°C)

**New Hampshire**
Capital: Concord
Statehood: June 21, 1788 (9th state)
Area: 8,969 square miles (23,231 sq km)
Nickname: The Granite State
State bird: Purple finch
State flower: Purple lilac
State tree: White birch
State song: "Old New Hampshire"
State motto: "Live free or die"
Average January temperature: 20°F (-7°C)
Average July temperature: 70°F (21°C)

**Maine**
Capital: Augusta
Statehood: March 15, 1820 (23rd state)
Area: 30,865 square miles (79,939 sq km)
Nicknames: Pine Tree State
State bird: Chickadee
State flower: White pine cone and tassel
State tree: White pine tree
State song: "State of Maine Song"
State motto: *Dirigo* ("I lead")
Average January temperature: 22°F (-6°C)
Average July temperature: 68°F (20°C)

THE RUGGED, ROMANTIC NEW ENGLAND COAST STRETCHES from the wealthy enclaves of Connecticut in the burgeoning shadow of New York City, meanders through four more seafaring states, and ends in a string of modest Maine fishing villages near the Canadian border. The distance seems modest as U.S. regions go, but appearances are deceiving. Innumerable bays and coves, river inlets, and inhabited islands stretch a visit to the region to several days. If the distance was measured by an imaginary string and somehow pulled tight, the Maine Coast, for example, would be longer than the whole California coastline.

The nation's drive for independence, its industrial revolution, "Yankee ingenuity," higher education, and the tradition of religious tolerance all began on or near the rocky New England shore. So did the country's first summer resorts, several enduring styles of architecture, the world's greatest fishing and whaling fleets, and the lives of four U.S. presidents. The West Indies and China trade began at Connecticut ports in the 1700s, as did the insurance industry after merchants agreed to share the losses when one of their ships was lost or commandeered by pirates.

Sandy beaches abound, especially in the southern New England states, but they are less the attraction here than along most other coastlines. The cold waters of the northern Atlantic and the abundance of dangerous rocks keep many bathers away from the surf. What draws the world to the New England shore are its sights: craggy cliffs, shifting dunes, forested islands a stone's throw from shore, lime-green salt marshes and their attendant wildlife, fabulous homes and yachts of the rich and famous, and oystermen at work and fishing boats bobbing in narrow coves.

Equally alluring is the palpable connection with American history at spots like Plymouth Rock, which is actually just a piece of a boulder where separatists called Pilgrims are said to have first set foot in the New World in 1620. Appealing, too, are the churches and assembly halls still standing in Boston where patriots stoked the embers of revolution. Interesting sites are endless: the docks of Nantucket and New Bedford in Massachusetts, where great whaling expeditions set off on journeys that lasted three years or more; the mighty shipyards of Bath in Maine; and the incredible living-history museums in Mystic, Connecticut, and Portsmouth, New Hampshire. In New Haven, Connecticut; Fall River, Massachusetts; Pawtucket, Rhode Island; and dozens more cities on the seashore or just up coastal rivers, vibrant textile, shoe, and furniture mills harnessed the power of water and steam, and their legacies live on for visitors to see.

Captain John Smith explored the coast of Massachusetts in 1614—six years before the Pilgrims landed at Provincetown and Plymouth. He called the lands before him "New England" and drew a map. Back in England, Prince Charles crossed out many of the Native American names and substituted English ones like "Cape Ann." By the time the Pilgrims, who were separatists seeking to escape the influence of the Church of England, arrived in 1620, the population of native Wampanoag, Nauset, and Pennacook Indians—once considered too hostile to permit white colonization—had been reduced by plagues introduced by English explorers, so colonization proceeded unfettered.

Other Englishmen set up their own chartered colonies in Salem and elsewhere on the Massachusetts coast in the 1620s, followed by the Puritans, Church of England zealots, who founded the Massachusetts Bay Company and settled what became Boston. By 1640, more than fifteen thousand settlers had taken up residence on the New England Coast. In 1691 separate colonies

*Artist Kate Huntington of Providence, Rhode Island, is a masterly painter of New England coastal scenes. This oil on canvas of the Victorian-era Surf Hotel on Block Island captures the indolent appeal of Rhode Island's relatively undiscovered vacation retreat. The painting was exhibited at Block Island's Mixed Media Gallery in New Harbor.*

*Impresario Phineas T. Barnum wintered his "Greatest Show on Earth" animals in his adopted hometown of Bridgeport, Connecticut. Here, elephants and citizens mass on the new Stratford Avenue Bridge to prove its strength.*

in Maine and Plymouth were joined to the Massachusetts Colony to form the Province of Massachusetts—though between Maine and lower Massachusetts along the Atlantic lay a sliver of a separate New Hampshire royal colony. To the south of Massachusetts in Rhode Island, the religiously tolerant colony founded by Roger Williams, who had been expelled from Salem, was prospering. Connecticut, having combined several small colonies into one, had its own royal charter as well.

Massachusetts prospered until the 1760s when Britain imposed the harsh Stamp and Sugar acts. These taxed the colony's publications and lucrative Triangle Trade, respectively. In the latter, lumber, salted fish, and livestock were sent to the West Indies where they were exchanged for sugar and molasses. The molasses was made into rum, which was traded for African slaves. The slaves were then sold to New England (and other) traders for gold. Massachusetts led the colonies' rebellion against restrictive measures from London, even organizing a boycott of British goods. When Parliament passed the Tea Act in 1773, allowing East India Company agents to undercut the price of tea then commanded by colonial importers, Boston townsmen disguised as Indians dumped a cargo of British tea into the harbor. Britain retaliated against the "Boston Tea Party" by passing still more restrictive measures, and in 1775 outright war against British rule broke out in Lexington and Concord, outside Boston. Following the Battle of Bunker Hill in Charlestown, won by the British at the cost of more than one thousand casualties, George Washington took command of Colonial forces at Cambridge, and the War of Independence was on in earnest. The British voluntarily abandoned Boston, and most of the fighting took place inland or south of New England, but rebel privateers sailing from New England ports menaced the British Navy at every turn. After the war, Massachusetts' own constitution, which was largely the work of John Adams and included both a list of citizen rights and a system of checks and balances among branches of government, helped inspire the new American nation's own Constitution and Bill of Rights.

Rhode Island ports welcomed New England's most diverse cast of immigrants: English Quakers and French Protestants as well as Sephardic Jews from Portugal, all seeking religious freedom during the Colonial period; French Canadians, Cape Verdeans, Swedes, and Catholic Portuguese to work the fishing and whaling trades; and Poles, Russians, Greeks, Hispanics, and southern blacks seeking work in the textile mills. It is little wonder that Rhode Island has been called an "ethnic laboratory."

Travel and recreation became an industry along the New England coast, too, at clusters of summer "cottages" (e.g. opulent mansions) such as Newport, Rhode Island; still more palatial resorts like Bar Harbor, Maine; at cities with an amazing historical heritage like Boston and steamship ports such as Fall River, Massachusetts; and at rollicking amusement parks like Savin Rock in New Haven, Connecticut, and Old Orchard Beach in Maine.

Of course the whole coastline, starting with picturesque Connecticut, in the southwest corner of New England, is an appealing visitor destination. Connecticut is easily the nation's wealthiest state as measured by per capita personal income, federal income taxes paid, and assessed value of real estate per capita. Its prosperity has created dynamic tensions along the coast, where prosperous gated communities, private islands, and restricted beaches are interspersed with aging cities like Bridgeport and New Haven that are struggling to deal with thorny economic and social problems. America's third-smallest state ranks fourth in population density, so rampant urban sprawl competes with Connecticut's ever-increasing gentrification. Within the Nutmeg State's thick forests live thousands of families whose breadwinners work out of state, especially in New York or Providence or even Boston. These commuters—many of whom live on fabulous country estates where farmhouses and barns no longer have any agricultural role—and the immigrants, who moved to the state to work in the mills and factories, together have inexorably drawn attention away from the sea. New Haven, for instance, was chosen for

*In 1900, Stonington, Connecticut, was a busy fishing port and the hub of a thriving steamboat business. The trains on seventeen tracks from New England cities and resorts connected with boats to New York.*

settlement by the Puritans because of its deep harbor, and ambitious seafaring expeditions left from there for many decades. Over time, however, industrialization and the growth of Yale University overshadowed the city's seafaring influence.

Communities along Long Island Sound developed slowly as tourist attractions. Much of the Connecticut coast and many offshore islands, including the Thimbles off Pine Orchard, are privately owned, but the state does operate large coastal parks near Westport, Madison, and East Lyme. They offer fine sandy beaches, but out-of-state visitors have traditionally bypassed them on their way to better-known vacation destinations in nearby states.

Urbanization damaged many coastal marshlands, and pollution degraded the Connecticut, Thames, and Naugatuck river networks. Shad and salmon runs up the 410-mile-long Connecticut—which was derided as the nation's "best-landscaped sewer"—ended by the 1950s. Eventually the state imposed some of the nation's strictest environmental controls, and citizens took action as well. Individuals and small organizations joined to form the Connecticut River Watershed

*The Breakers, one of the most resplendent "cottages" in Newport, Rhode Island, was rebuilt after a fire for Cornelius Vanderbilt by Richard Morris Hunt. The Renaissance-style palace is Rhode Island's leading tourist attraction.*

Council, which has helped restore tidelands, wildlife preserves, and water quality along the *Queneh-ta-cut*—the Native American word for "the beautiful river." By 1998, the Connecticut was clean enough to be named by President Bill Clinton as one of fourteen "American Heritage River" systems across the United States.

Away from the bigger coastal cities like Bridgeport and New Haven, the Connecticut coastline is rich in green space, history, and quaintness. "Expect to make lots of hairpin turns and get hopelessly lost on shore loop roads," write Parke Puterbaugh and Alan Bisbort in their *Life Is a Beach* vacationers' guide. "Then suddenly you'll round a corner and find yourself in a well-groomed, picture-postcard village by the sea." The authors loved old Mystic harbor, where they found lots of variety among souvenirs: "Scrimshaw, Harpoons, Tee Shirts, Rose Bracelets, Salt Water Taffy."

Greenwich, the city that authors Barbara Clayton and Kathleen Whitley have called the "portal to New England's coast," might better be labeled as the entryway to a rarefied gold coast of snug communities in the sprawling orbit of New York City. Greenwich has managed to retain its colonial charm, ample green space, and quiet streets lined with great homes while reluctantly absorbing corporate headquarters, clogged highways, and commuter rail lines. How reluctantly? In his 1976 book on the New England states, Neil R. Peirce wrote that while more than one hundred New York corporations moved to Greenwich in 1970 and 1971 alone—contributing more than $2 million a year in taxes without adding many demands on city services—that "the residents of Greenwich were not enthusiastic. They had moved there to avoid the city and didn't want the city to follow them."

East along Long Island Sound, Norwalk's rich history as the source of small, delicious oysters that are prized throughout New England is maintained in an annual oyster festival. The sound's

marine life and habitats are depicted at the Maritime Aquarium located in a beautifully restored nineteenth-century foundry near the heart of South Norwalk's old oystering community. A deteriorating warehouse district has come alive as a busy arts scene where loft studios, art galleries, and one of the region's finest maritime centers are enticing people back downtown.

It was in Bridgeport that the nation's first sewing machine and gramophones were produced, and P.T. Barnum organized his "Greatest Show on Earth" there during its heyday. Barnum once had not one but *four* mansions in town—and great museums filled with curiosities in several cities. Most of the museums were wooden and burned, never to be rebuilt. Inside the Romanesque 1891 Barnum Museum in Bridgeport—built to house the city's Institute of Science and History—Barnum's circus career is remembered with displays of jovial midget Tom Thumb's life, a display about Barnum's promotion of "Swedish Nightingale" Jenny Lind, and an incredible one-thousand-square-foot moving scale model of a three-ring circus with half a million pieces that was carved over sixty years by William Brinley. Bridgeport's own rich history as a center of cigar-, corset-, and buttonmaking is also imaginatively portrayed.

Connecticut has one of the better records among states when it comes to preserving its colorful past. Its coastal area once consisted of a number of tiny, independent Puritan colonies, including New Haven, Saybrook, and New London. Once unified, Connecticut brazenly claimed territory west to the Pacific Ocean. Territory as far away as northeastern Ohio, for instance, was aggressively surveyed and settled by agents operating on a Connecticut charter. Connecticut's seafaring traditions trace to the Revolutionary War when its privateers wreaked havoc on British supply vessels. The period of prosperity along the Connecticut coast in the mid-nineteenth century—when the port of Mystic built many of the vessels that would sail for the Union Navy in the American Civil

*At its old location in downtown Plymouth, Massachusetts, Plimoth Plantation historic interpreters dressed as visitors expected Pilgrims to look. Costumes and activities are historically correct at the relocated site outside of town.*

War—has been meticulously recreated at Mystic Seaport. There, the collection of ship models, figureheads, carvings, and small craft honor the great boat designers and builders of a time gone by. Connecticut would also be a key "arsenal of democracy" in World War II when more than seventy submarines were built in Groton. (Connecticut had been an arsenal of a different sort years earlier, too, when Winchester rifles rolled out of New Haven and Colt pistols out of Hartford.)

Cultural oases are also plentiful along the Connecticut shore. Yale University's art galleries and museum of natural history are world-renowned. In Guilford is the Henry Whitfield House, perhaps the oldest surviving stone house in the nation, which is now a state museum. In architecturally rich towns like Madison and Guilford, Old Saybrook, Niantic, Old Lyme, and Noank, many tidy old homes have been turned into museums, bookshops, historical association headquarters, and bed-and-breakfast inns. New London, which once ranked behind only New Bedford, Massachusetts, as a world whaling center, has dozens of homes listed on the National Register of Historic Places, including four Greek Revival houses on "Whale Oil Row." The United States Coast

*Future president John F. Kennedy, then twenty-seven in 1944, recuperated at his family's compound in Hyannisport, Massachusetts, after his PT-109 craft was sunk by a Japanese destroyer in the Pacific.*

Guard Academy, based on a bucolic 125-acre campus along the Thames River in New London, got its start as a training academy aboard a schooner, then a barque, in the 1870s.

So important is the sea to neighboring Rhode Island, the nation's smallest state, that its license plates carry the nickname "The Ocean State." That is ocean as in family beaches and pleasant little fishing towns—not to mention beautiful Narragansett Bay, whose waters and nearly four hundred miles of ragged coastline are its most significant natural treasure. Even bustling Providence has rediscovered its harbor—once a pillar of the Triangle Trade with the West Indies and Europe—around which an eclectic arts and cultural scene has been established. "Renaissance City," the national newspaper *USA Today* called the Rhode Island state capital.

Florentine navigator Giovanni da Verrazzano, sailing for France, gave the entire state (which is not an island) its name when he likened Block Island, when he came upon it in 1524, to Rhodes in the Mediterranean Sea. At one time Rhode Island was the nation's most industrialized state, but as mills and factories closed in blue-collar cities like Woonsocket, tourism relating to the sea has grown in importance. Newport, one of America's first summer playgrounds for the idle rich, alone attracts thousands of visitors who gawk at the rows of resplendent "cottages" that line the coast.

Within the one hundred miles of beaches in South County, Rhode Island—the waterfront region that stretches between the Connecticut line and Newport and includes Watch Hill, Misquamicut, and Ninigret—are some of the largest, warmest, and most diverse attractions in New England. South County does not exist on a map; it is the term for this entire southern Rhode Island area where the living is easy. A guide to Rhode Island beaches grows repetitive. One after the other, they are described as "sandy," "clean," "pretty," and "popular with families." The publication might have added "jammed." Misquamicut even has designated areas for board and body surfing. Families from throughout the region are increasingly discovering the carousels—including the nation's oldest "flying horse" carousel in Westerly—water slides, lighthouses, ruins of old forts, boardwalks, and coves full of fishing boats; and just across the highway from more than one Rhode Island beach are salt ponds and nature preserves. On Narragansett Beach are landmark towers, all that is left of a massive oceanfront casino designed by the New York architectural firm of McKim, Mead, and White that burned in 1910. The state maintains more than fifty recreation areas—many along the shoreline—and at several places on "Little Rhody's" coast, state beaches butt up against town parks and beaches. In little Charlestown alone—where surf fishing for "blues" is among the best in America—there are four beaches to choose from. The Green Trail of South County connects such sites as the Galilee Salt Marsh, Quonochontaug Breachway (a birder's paradise), and Narragansett Pier. Fishing in places like Watch Hill is more local color than a significant part of the state economy, for fishing, lobstering, and agriculture combined account for less than 2 percent of Rhode Island's labor force.

There are thirty-five small islands in Rhode Island's Narragansett Bay. And on Block Island, fifteen miles offshore, visitors can step back into the Victorian age at hotels that date to the 1880s, wander marshlands and stroll past freshwater ponds, or soak up history that recalls the days of pirates, smugglers, and naval bombardments as far back as the Revolutionary War. The Nature Conservancy has designated Block Island "one of the last great places in the Western Hemisphere."

Moving east to southern Massachusetts, one can admire some remarkable preservationist accomplishments. In New Bedford, for example—once the world's whaling capital and still among the nation's leading fishing ports—the harbor is now a fascinating historic district. There, whaling ships were refitted between lengthy journeys out to sea, and barrels of whale oil lined the wharves. The National Park Service oversees the district and provides an information center, but individual elements like the New Bedford Whaling Museum and a sailors' chapel called a "seamen's bethel" are independent attractions. Inside the whaling museum, in addition to figureheads, harpoons and whale skeletons, and paintings and photographs from the

*On August 5, 1910, President Taft and Mrs. Taft arrive to dedicate the Pilgrim Memorial Monument, commemorating the Pilgrims' landing in Provincetown, on Massachusetts' Cape Cod, before they sailed to Plymouth.*

*Nathaniel Hawthorne often visited his cousin, Suzannah Ingersoll, at her home in Salem, Massachusetts. He set his novel,* The House of Seven Gables, *there. The house was opened to tours in 1910.*

days when whale oil lit the lamps of America, is the *Lagoda*, the world's largest ship's model. It is a half-scale replica of an actual square-rigger that sailed from New Bedford.

On January 3 of each year, the whaling museum stages a marathon reading of Herman Melville's *Moby Dick*. Visitors take turns reading from the story of Melville's own four-year expedition on the whaler *Acushnet* that left from nearby Fairhaven, Massachusetts, on January 3, 1841. This continuous reading lasts about twenty-four hours.

Nearby Fall River, too, has retained the look of authenticity from the days when it was both a factory town and an important steamship and excursion-boat port. Hundreds of huge factories and textile mills—some abandoned and others creatively converted to other uses—loom over the harbor. Before technology enabled engineers to build railroad bridges across coastline channels, trains ran between Boston and Fall River, and then magnificently appointed steamships carried passengers on to New York. Today Fall River is home to Battleship Cove, where two U.S. battleships—including the USS *Massachusetts*—and a World War II attack submarine are open for tours. On Buzzards Bay, the western gateway to Cape Cod, are three coastal villages—Mattapoisett, Marion, and Wareham—where the legend of the sea lives on in great captains' houses and merchants' homes.

It was at scorpion-shaped Cape Cod that the Pilgrims first touched land at what is now Provincetown in 1620—eighteen years after English explorer Bartholomew Gosnold discovered the peninsula and named it for the plentiful codfish in the waters offshore. The Pilgrims stayed around for just five weeks before sailing on to Plymouth. It was while anchored off this little spit of Cape Cod that they signed the Mayflower Compact. Having been forced by storms to land several hundred miles north of their intended destination in Virginia—thus sending them into

uncharted territory outside English governmental authority—the Pilgrims decided to draw up "Laws, Ordinances, Acts, Constitutions, and Offices" that would bind Pilgrims and non-Pilgrims alike in a "Civil Body Politic" once they found a suitable harbor at which to go ashore. The compact stipulated rule by majority (thus keeping non-Pilgrim settlers in their place) and rule by the people themselves rather than a distant king. Pilgrims later returned to Cape Cod, where today all but two towns have English names and two-thirds are named after English seaports.

The Cape is part of the mainland, but the scenic Cape Cod Canal, which connects Buzzards and Cape Cod bays, has effectively turned it into an island. Certainly visitors revel in its splendid isolation after negotiating the snaillike drive over the Bourne and Sagamore bridges to their Cape destinations on a summer Friday afternoon or Saturday morning. There is a saying on Cape Cod that once you visit and get sand in your shoes, you'll return, and thousands of New Englanders do each summer. Sand is plentiful on the beaches, in the wild dunes, and along the salt ponds of the Cape Cod National Seashore. In fact it was mounds of sand, carried northward by fast-moving ocean currents, that formed the Outer Cape's scorpion's tail, or fishhook, that juts northward into the Atlantic from Eastham to Wellfleet and on to Provincetown.

Classic, shingled cottages along the shore and among the peninsula's pines are a quintessential Cape Cod attraction all their own. Other popular sites range from the gristmill and historic glassmaking studios in Sandwich to the 1793 windmill in Eastham to the John F. Kennedy Memorial overlooking Lewis Bay in Hyannis and the Kennedy Hyannis Museum downtown, as well as the classic New England greens in Falmouth, the antique shops all along meandering Route 6A on the northern shore, the art galleries and the giant Pilgrim Tower monument in Provincetown, Chatham's railroad museum and a fire museum in Brewster, and the

*Residents of Salem, Massachusetts, at the turn of the century, enjoy the Collins Cove beach at the foot of Arabella Street. The beach is still in use, but bathing attire has changed radically.*

lighthouses all around the cape. In Mashpee—a town still administered by the Wampanoag Tribe that once controlled the entire peninsula—an annual powwow featuring tribal dances, a "fireball game," and a traditional clambake—attracts Native Americans as well as other visitors from many states each Fourth of July weekend. Little wonder Cape Cod's year-round population of two hundred thousand or so more than triples each summer.

This region is where "getting away from it all" has become a New England art form. It is often referred to as Cape Cod *and the Islands*, meaning also Nantucket and Martha's Vineyard in the open ocean south of the cape. Nantucket, where the American whaling industry was born in the early nineteenth century before larger whaling vessels shifted operations to New Bedford's deeper harbor, is full of wild and foggy heathlands, cranberry bogs, flowered hedgerows, aquafarms and wildlife refuges, cedar-shingle cottages and tiny gardens, guest houses and luxury hotels, bookstores and bicycle paths, and white sandy beaches. Nantucket has its own whaling museum and even a lifesaving museum as well.

Larger Martha's Vineyard, named by explorer Gosnold in honor of his baby daughter and the profusion of wild grapes he found on the island, offers even more charms including the occasional spotting of one of the many celebrities who summer or visit there. In Oak Bluffs there is an amazing array of little "carpenter gothic," or gingerbread-trimmed, houses built around an old Methodist campground and assembly hall. Elegant Edgartown, home to stately Greek Revival houses, is a world-famous yachting center and the gateway, via a little three-car ferry, to the tiny adjacent island of Chappaquiddick, which the locals call "Chappy." There one finds a wild, grassy beach and a spectacular lighthouse, reachable by car only after first deflating one's tires to fifteen pounds of pressure in order to navigate the deep, sandy paths. Vineyard Haven is the mercantile center, with a mix of boutiques, jewelry stores, book shops, and tiny restaurants. If this settlement in the middle of the island represents refined civilization, Gay Head on the Vineyard's western tip brings out all that is natural on the island. There is a wildlife preserve called "Noman's Land" and multicolored limestone cliffs formed over millions of years. From the majestic cliffs one can see the distant, mostly uninhabited Elizabeth Islands.

*The White Island Lighthouse stands on one of four Isles of Shoals in New Hampshire waters. Rebuilt in 1857, it was reinforced with steel bands in the 1860s and fully automated in 1987.*

Massachusetts' South Shore between Cape Cod and Boston includes a necklace of attractive bedroom communities, tiny yacht basins, and municipal and state parks. The biggest attraction is Plymouth, which is sometimes called "America's hometown." An old Pilgrim graveyard, the stone that is said to be Plymouth Rock, and *Mayflower II*—an exact replica of the first Pilgrim ship that is part of Plimoth Plantation's operation—are all downtown. The remainder of the plantation, which is a reconstruction of the Pilgrims' original settlement, lies outside of town. There, costumed interpreters speak early English amongst themselves and to visitors while demonstrating tasks such as barn raising and soap making. Up the coast in Quincy is the Adams National Historic Site, which includes the birth homes of presidents John and John Quincy Adams, and the family home where the father and son both later lived.

The invigorating city of Boston nearly lost touch with the sea as it grew into New England's dominant commercial and financial center, and government activities coalesced around the Boston Common and Beacon Hill. Many of the city's old wharves have been brought back to

life as waterfront restaurants, shops, hotels and condominiums. The New England Aquarium sits at the end of the old Central Wharf, in the shadow of downtown, and the John F. Kennedy Memorial Library overlooks Boston Harbor. The narrow streets of Boston's oldest neighborhood, the North End, recall the days of massive Irish, Jewish, and especially Italian immigration; and seafaring books, maps, and antiques are plentiful along Charles Street on Beacon Hill. The Charles River, leading from Boston Harbor, connects the city's splendid Museum of Science to two of the nation's greatest institutions of higher learning—Harvard University and the Massachusetts Institute of Technology. Boston's tie to the sea is maintained, too, in Charlestown at the old Navy Yard, where "Old Ironsides," the USS *Constitution*—the oldest commissioned ship in the U.S. Navy—is moored between its occasional sallies forth into Boston Harbor. The *Constitution* never lost a battle in its forays during the campaign against North Africa's Barbary Pirates in the early nineteenth century and in the War of 1812 against the British Navy.

It was on Massachusetts' North Shore, especially around Gloucester—the nation's oldest seaport—on Cape Ann, which reaches outward into the Atlantic, that the image of the intrepid New England fisherman took root. Beginning almost four centuries ago, boats based here set sail in search of cod, haddock, and other cold-water whitefish. It is a salty tradition that is marked each Labor Day weekend by the Great Schooner Race. The *Washington Post* has called the event "a nautical Mardi Gras," since Gloucester, the newspaper cleverly noted, has become a "drinking town with a fishing problem." That is because of the city's economic struggles that were brought on by the depletion of the North Atlantic catch due to overfishing. Gloucester's waterfront is still active, however. A promenade there is still watched over by the 1923 statue of a mariner at the wheel, dedicated to those lost at sea. In Gloucester, too, is Rocky Neck, the nation's oldest active artists' colony.

*The Samoset Resort in Rockport, Maine, was originally built as the Bay Point Hotel on Penobscot Bay and later renamed for a Pemaquid Indian who greeted the Mayflower Pilgrims. In 1974, it was lavishly rebuilt after a devastating fire.*

*Workers (circa 1920) plank a schooner-barge at the Kelley-Spear shipyard in Bath, Maine. It was the last wooden ship-yard in Bath and built its last vessel in 1923.*

Nearby Salem has a long seafaring tradition as well; indeed many of its early leaders made millions of dollars on trade with the Far East, and their fine Federal-style homes can be found in several parts of town. But Salem is far better known for the witch-hunting hysteria that swept this Puritan colony in the late 1600s. In town, there is a witch house where accused witches were questioned before some were hanged; a witch museum; a wax museum where witches again steal the show; a dungeon museum where actors portray witches; and even a logo on the police department's patrol cars showing witches on broomsticks. Just to add to the spookiness is the mysterious House of Seven Gables—a landmark complete with a secret staircase—that was once owned by Nathaniel Hawthorne's cousin. The author made the house famous in his dark novel of the same name.

Great houses with widow's walks are plentiful in Newburyport, Rockport, and other North Shore towns as well, as the captains of clipper ships built fine homes near the sea. There is a shipbuilding museum in Essex, rows of seventeenth-century houses in Ipswitch, salt marshes near Rowley, and a long spit of barrier-beach dunes and both fresh and saltwater marshes on Plum Island.

New Hampshire's short stretch of seashore—just eighteen miles long—is a place of incredible contrast. There is a quiet, state-owned swimming beach near Rye and New Castle. Hampton Beach includes a three-mile boardwalk, amusement park, and seven-acre "casino"—not a gambling establishment but an entertainment arcade and ballroom. And then there is graceful, historic Portsmouth, one of the best-preserved maritime centers in New England. Admiral John Paul Jones, who uttered the famous line, "I have not yet begun to fight," aboard the *Bonhomme Richard* while locked in battle with the British frigate *Serapis* during the Revolutionary War, owned a fine home—now a museum—in Portsmouth. For nearly two centuries, the Portsmouth Naval Shipyard turned out vessels, including submarines, that ranged across the Seven Seas. In Portsmouth, too, is Strawbery Banke, a remarkable cluster of buildings saved from ruination by a spirited civic organization. It is a restored, ten-acre waterfront museum where one can find everything from an array of Colonial homes and gardens to a 1940s corner store.

Maine's 3,478 miles of coastline are so remote in spots that only a small percentage can be seen from a highway. By boat, however, one can sail past undeveloped coves, sleepy fishing villages, the notorious rocks and boulders that line the shore and jut from the surf, and approximately 3,500 inhabited and uninhabited offshore islands.

The southern Maine coast features a surprising string of white sandy beaches in York, Ogunquit, Wells, Kennebunk, Saco, and Old Orchard. So wide and hard-packed is Old Orchard's beach, in fact, that Charles Lindbergh once landed his *Spirit of St. Louis* there. But the area draws even more visitors for another activity: shopping. Kittery—an old shipbuilding town barely an hour north of Boston—got its first discount store in 1938 and is now loaded with more than 125 national and regional outlet stores in thirteen separate malls, making it a contender for the Outlet Capital of the nation. Everything from candles to china to flags has its own discount shop. Already crowded, Kittery becomes virtually impassable on Memorial Day weekend and towards the end of summer when sidewalk sales add to the "shop-'til-you-drop" frenzy. And Freeport, a town of 7,200 that was also once a shipbuilding center just north of Portland, has grown as a shopping mecca attracting almost four million visitors a year. The town is the home of L.L. Bean, the world-famous, twenty-four-hour-a-day mail-order company whose outdoor store is now flanked by dozens of other specialty stores and outlets. Freeport, where the treaty separating Maine from Massachusetts was signed in 1820, has tried to hold onto its small-town character in the face of rampant expansion. Even the local McDonald's fast-food outlet is located in a historic house.

Maine calls itself "Vacationland," and many a vacation includes a "blast from the past" at the historic amusement park at Old Orchard Beach; an antiquing foray to York—the first chartered city in America; a walk along secluded paths among sixteen hundred acres of wetlands of the Rachel Carson National Wildlife Refuge; or a stroll through an auto museum in Wells, a brick store museum in Kennebunk, or a museum that houses the world's largest collections of trolleys in Kennebunkport.

Maine's largest city, Portland, is small enough—with a population barely over sixty thousand—to explore comfortably. Indeed, only Burlington, Vermont, and Charleston, West Virginia, are smaller among the largest cities of the various states. Portland attractions include the Old Port Exchange waterfront district, a top-ranked art museum and hands-on children's museum, an arts district crammed with galleries and studios, elegant hotels, and luxurious mansions, including the boyhood home of poet Henry Wadsworth Longfellow. In the 1600s, John Smith reported back to his superiors in England that Casco Bay, which spreads before present-day Portland, had "as many islands as there are days in the year." Thus these are known as the "Calendar Islands," though Smith overcounted them by 229 (230 in a leap year!).

From Portland and Freeport to the New Brunswick border, the Maine coast turns more eastward than north; hence the term "Downeast Maine." Mainers, or "Mainiacs" as they are fond of calling themselves,

*Ships have been built in Bath, Maine, since 1607. Here, in the late 1930s, workers install rivets in welded seams. The town's iron works still turn out U.S. Navy and merchant ships.*

have a harder time explaining the "down" part of the expression, as one is still heading *up* the Atlantic Coast. The state's Mid-Coast region is dotted with seaside villages, broad bays, thriving resort towns, and little lobstering ports. (Almost 90 percent of the lobsters caught in America are harvested in Maine.)

The "prettiest village in Maine," by its own declaration, is Wiscasset, and its stately sea captains' mansions, sumptuous antique galleries, and colorful narrow-gauge railroad certainly put it in the running for the title. Other candidates would be Boothbay and Boothbay Harbor, famous for their art exhibits, antique shows, band concerts, fishing and whale-watching excursions, and restaurants. The Mid-Coast offers many opportunities for a different kind of culinary experience as well. It is a lobster feast "in the rough," which usually means an inexpensive pile of the steamed crustaceans served on paper plates laid on picnic tables. Sometimes you also get a drink and cole slaw, sometimes you don't. From Port Clyde one can take a mail boat, year-round, to Monhegan Island ten miles offshore. No cars are allowed there; it is a quiet place with footpaths, sylvan forests, and ample ocean views. Thus, artists are among the frequent visitors.

Maine is home to one of the nation's most beautiful—and most visited—national wonders. It is Acadia National Park, which is spread over Mount Desert Island and the Schoodic Peninsula, as well as Isle au Haut and the Cranberry Islands offshore. Created in 1916, Acadia is the nation's oldest national park east of the Mississippi River. At the summit of the park's Cadillac Mountain on a clear day, one can see Mount Katahdin, the starting point of the Appalachian Trail ninety miles to the north. Spread out directly below, as well, is the whole of beautiful Bar Harbor.

Bar Harbor was a grand resort city with magnificent mansions and rooms for five thousand visitors arriving by rail, yacht, and steamboat in the years before and after the turn of the twentieth century. Increased automobile travel and the Great Depression put a crimp in business, and a devastating fire in 1947—in which five great hotels and more than two hundred grand homes and summer cottages were leveled—ruined the resort. But fine restaurants and galleries, and boating on Frenchman Bay, not to mention the town's proximity to Acadia National Park, have brought back the tourists. Other notable stops along the Mid-Coast: the dock in Castine,

*Power boats were already popular at the Boothbay Harbor Yacht Club in Maine in 1913, less than twenty years after the introduction of marine engines. Organized in 1907, the club still exists.*

where the *State of Maine*, the huge training ship for the Maine Maritime Academy, is usually anchored; Blue Hill, where acclaimed potters keep their shops and numerous chamber musicians summer and give concerts; Deer Isle, known for its crafts thanks to the presence of the Haystack Mountain School of Crafts; and Bucksport, a deep-water anchorage that is home to Fort Knox. Not *that* Fort Knox, but a massive granite fortification, full of tunnels, built in 1844.

Incredibly, a number of maps and guidebooks of the New England Coast simply end at Bar Harbor as if nothing of consequence existed in the lands beyond. Taking this cue, relatively few tourists venture into the *real* Downeast Maine from the Schoodic Peninsula to the New Brunswick border. They are missing a throwback world of hardworking fishing families, blueberry barrens, dense woods, fish hatcheries, moose bogs, and international parks and bridges. They are also missing the fascinating admixture of Yankee reticence and French Canadian *joie de vivre*. The "Old Sow," the largest tidal whirlpool in the Western Hemisphere, lies within view of the car ferry route between Eastport and Deer Island. The nation's most easterly city (Eastport) and town

(Lubec) can be found Downeast, and thus the spectacular sunrises for which the area is known arrive here before the sun can be seen anywhere else in America—six hours before the first rays can be seen in Hawaii. One more geographical footnote: the little town of Perry, just below the Canadian border, lies exactly halfway between the North Pole and the equator. And a meteorological factoid: High tide on Passamaquoddy Bay, twenty-eight feet, is the highest in the country.

Across the Roosevelt International Bridge from Lubec is Campobello Island, Canadian territory that is home to a unique international park. The longtime summer home of Franklin Roosevelt and his family as well as adjoining cottages once owned by wealthy Americans are part of a compound jointly run and equally staffed by Canadians and Americans. The site, where Roosevelt began his battle with polio in 1921 and where Eleanor Roosevelt summered (and wrote her autobiography) long after her husband was otherwise occupied in Washington, is the only known park in one country that honors a great leader of another.

Towns like Lubec and Calais and Machias in Maine's "Sunrise County" are struggling. Fishing or raking blueberries is not lucrative enough to bring prosperity Downeast or to keep most young people at home. There are no outlet malls, department stores, chain motels, or fancy boutiques here; indeed, grocery stores struggle to stay open. Yet you ask a lobsterman why he hauls up traps on days when winds are howling and ice clings to his line, and he gives the same answer that you get when you ask a Cape Cod "regular" why she fights the traffic on the Sagamore roundabout each weekend, or an executive who commutes to Manhattan every day from home on the Connecticut shore why he puts up with the aggravation. The answer: "Because it's what I know. It's part of me, something I'm comfortable with." And because the rewards— the sea, the air, the serenity, the friends—are worth the trouble. The craggy coast of New England is like that: comfortable, serene, and worth getting to.

A single estate once covered Greenwich Point in Greenwich, which is located less than fifty miles from downtown Manhattan on Connecticut's southwestern coast. Now residents enjoy gardens (top right) and beaches at a gated park here. Greenwich is home to many corporations whose leaders sought less frenzied surroundings close—but not too close—to "the City." The Barnum Museum (bottom right) in downtown Bridgeport, Connecticut, was opened in 1893, two years after the showman's death, as the Barnum Institute of Science and History. The museum's sometimes mischievous exhibits recall the impresario, his legendary circus, his promotions of "Swedish nightingale" Jenny Lind and midget "General" Tom Thumb, and Barnum's philanthropy in Bridgeport. Yale University (opposite) was chartered in 1701 as "The Collegiate School." Its activities are a vital economic engine in New Haven, Connecticut.

The Old Lighthouse (above) has become the headquarters of the Historical Society of Stonington, Connecticut. It includes a museum of lighthouse history and lore. Storms and shore erosion took their toll on the thirty-foot stone tower, and in 1840 the structure was dismantled, and its materials used to build a new tower and keeper's dwelling on higher ground. The light remained active until 1889 when a beacon was installed on the town breakwater. Yale University was founded in 1701 at the salt box-style Buckingham House (right) in Old Saybrook, Connecticut, before moving operations to New Haven fifteen years later. Some original shake shingles remain on the house.

The wealthy and famous live in homes—some of which take up most of an entire island—on the Thimble Islands (left) offshore from Branford, Connecticut. Sightseeing boats pass among the 365 isles, some of which appear within touching distance of shore. But residents assiduously guard their privacy. The islands were named for thimbleberries, which have thimble-shaped blackberry-like fruit that grow on some of them. The 1639 medieval-style Henry Whitfield House in Guilford (above), named for the town's founder and first minister, is the oldest stone house in New England. It is now a Connecticut state museum. Evidence that the house was built as a fort can be found in its walls, which slant outward and are eighteen inches thick at the top, thirty inches at the bottom.

Carved wooden ship's
figureheads (above)
and the whaleship
Charles W. Morgan
(right) are among
the attractions at the
nonprofit Mystic
Seaport, the nation's
largest maritime
museum. Located
on seventeen acres
along the Mystic River
in Connecticut, it
features more than
450 historic water-
craft, ships' fittings
and craft demonstra-
tions, and an amazing
scale model of the
river harbor and sur-
roundings. Old
Harbor (overleaf), on
Block Island in the
Rhode Island waters of
Long Island Sound, is
reached by ferry from
several coastal cities.
Once called "the Ber-
muda of the North,"
the remarkably open
Block Island is a
paradise of Victoriana
with vintage hotels
and homes, rugged
cliffs, and two mag-
nificent lighthouses.

Ferries to Block Island land at a settlement called New Harbor, where one finds "Rebecca" (opposite), the fountain named for the biblical Rebekah at the Well. It was erected, complete with a water-fountain pedestal, in 1896 by the Women's Christian Temperance Union in a failed effort to wean islanders from their liquor and beer. Disciples of demon rum delighted in pointing out that grape garlands adorn Rebecca's hair. Block Island's uncluttered landscape (overleaf) is enchanting. On the Rhode Island mainland between Charlestown and South Kingstown (above), beaches are inviting. All of South County (there is no such single county) earns its reputation as a place where "the living is easy." Surprisingly, Rhode Island's wide, family-oriented beaches, nostalgic arcades, and abundant wildlife refuges have remained almost hidden from the millions of travelers who pass them by on the way to better-publicized destinations.

The 1869 Rose Island Lighthouse (above), on a rocky island in the east passage of Rhode Island's lower Narragansett Bay, was long a family home as well as a sentinel station. Once a week, the lightkeeper would sail to Newport for provisions, towing a skiff. Now the house is the center of an environmental adventure. Guests in the unusual hostel and museum are accommodated in the keeper's old bedroom (opposite). But their electricity and water use is strictly monitored, and composting and beach clean-up are part of the daily routine. Staying at the lighthouse, says Charlotte Johnson, executive director of the foundation that renovated the once-abandoned and dilapidated facility, "is a mind-altering experience, without the drugs." Visitors still occasionally find remnants from the island's earlier days when it was a British, then French, fortification; quarantine for cholera victims; torpedo station; and ammunition dump.

Hammersmith Farm (opposite) was the childhood summer home of Jacqueline Bouvier Kennedy and the summer White House when she was First Lady from 1961 to 1963. John W. Auchincloss built the twenty-eight-room, shingle-style cottage in 1887. His son, Hugh D. Auchincloss, married Jacqueline Kennedy's divorced mother, and when Jacqueline wed John F. Kennedy in Newport in 1953, the reception was held at Hammersmith Farm. In contrast to the opulent, even outlandish, mansions in town along Bellevue Avenue, Hammersmith exudes rustic charm. Its deck room, for instance, is cozy and unpretentious, and furnishings throughout the house are practical as well as elegant. The farm— now Newport's only working spread—was established in 1640 by William Brenton of England. Its fifty rolling acres overlook the entrance to Newport Harbor on Narragansett Bay. Legendary landscape architect Frederick Law Olmsted originally designed the estate's terrace gardens (above).

It took four years, from 1888 through 1891, for Richard Morris Hunt to build the glittering Marble House, Newport's most elaborate summer house, for Mr. and Mrs. William K. Vanderbilt. Diners took their meals on solid bronze chairs by Allard of Paris (right) under an intricate gilt ceiling (above). Elsewhere, the stunning house featured a Gold Ballroom, a marble staircase, a ten-ton grille across the front entrance, a Gothic Room for the Vanderbilts' collection of miniatures and art objects, and several elaborate chandeliers—also by Allard. Harold S. Vanderbilt gave the house to the Newport County Historical Society in 1963. Battleship Cove (overleaf) in Heritage State Park in Fall River, Massachusetts, is a showplace of naval might. Most visited is a World War II battleship, the USS Massachusetts.

The HMS Bounty (opposite) from the movie Mutiny on the Bounty welcomes visitors at Fall River's Heritage State Park. Donated by cable-TV mogul Ted Turner, the ship features sixteen sails, six cannons, and ten miles of running rigging. Massachusetts' history as the world's greatest whaling port is commemorated at the New Bedford Whaling Museum. There, visitors can examine the whaling bark Lagoda (above) whose twelve long voyages netted her owners $652,000 in profit. Across the street is another part of the New Bedford Whaling National Historical Park—a seamen's bethel (left) or mariners' chapel. It includes tomblike monuments to men who lost their lives at sea.

Nostalgic Oak Bluffs on Martha's Vineyard Island off the Massachusetts coast was the site of Wesleyan Grove, the Methodist Church's first camp meeting ground. Summertime Sabbath meetings there in the 1850s drew twelve thousand worshipers. Rows of "carpenter gothic" filigreed cottages (right) surround the original open-air tabernacle. Visitors walk past homes like the six-room "Pink House" (above), built in 1867. Once barn-red, the cottage was painted a shocking pink in 1983. Oak Bluffs is also home to the Flying Horse Carousel, the nation's oldest operating carousel. Rugged clay cliffs (overleaf) at Gay Head on the eastern tip of Martha's Vineyard are a stark reminder of the power of the sea. One of the Vineyard's five lighthouses, located at Gay Head, often opens to tours.

Lighthouse buffs love Martha's Vineyard because it offers a diverse group of five lights in a limited, easily accessible area. At one time, more ships sailed through Vineyard Sound and Nantucket Sound, surrounding the island, than in any other place in the world but the English Channel. In 1938, the Edgartown Light (left) replaced an earlier structure on a small, manmade island, accessible only by boat or footbridge. Sand gradually filled the gap to the mainland, and the beautiful lighthouse now stands on shore. The little West Chop Light (above), a sentinel above Vineyard Haven's harbor, was built in 1817 and replaced by the present brick structure twenty-one years later. Twice, the structure had to be moved inland, away from the edge of a sixty-foot-high bluff.

Crescent-shaped Nantucket Island, thirty miles off Cape Cod, offers more than eight hundred buildings constructed before 1850 (above and right). As a result, the entire island is a national historic district that strictly polices its unspoiled beaches and solitary lighthouses. Nantucket Town is full of sea captains' Federal-style houses, unique shops, and epicurean restaurants. Byways are dotted with saltbox cottages clad in the island's distinctive gray shingles. Nantucket is renowned for its late-April Daffodil Festival, which celebrates the reawakening after a dozy winter. Each fall, the Garden Club gives daffodil bulbs to each island schoolchild whose plantings contribute to the bounty of three million blossoms come spring.

Sachem was a Wampanoag chieftain who guided white settlers to Hyannis on Cape Cod. A statue in his honor (above) rests on the Hyannis green, site of popular summer concerts. Visitors to nearby Hyannisport maneuver through labyrinthine streets in search of the Kennedy family compound, getting only so far (left) along the shore.

The array of Kennedy Family houses is visible only from offshore. Cape sunsets, as along Cook's Brook Beach in Eastham (overleaf), are spectacular. There is a saying that if you visit and get sand in your shoes, you will return. That is a virtual certainty since it is almost impossible to enjoy the Cape's delights and not walk a sandy beach.

*Forlorn dunes (above) weave throughout the Cape Cod National Seashore. The twenty-seven-thousand-acre ecotourist's paradise includes forty miles of sandy beaches as well as bike trails, nature paths, woods, and marshlands. At Orleans Harbor (right), plain and fancy boats dock together. In Truro, on the Cape's narrow fishhook-shaped spit, simple cottages (overleaf) carry floral names like "Primrose," "Marigold," and "Blueball." The Cape is a convenient weekend and summer-long retreat for residents throughout Massachusetts and eastern Rhode Island. Visitors who drive U.S. Highway 6 through the piney woods in the heart of the Cape might wonder what the fuss is about. The slower, but far more scenic old king's post road, Highway 6A, reveals treasures like windmills, fishing coves, artists' studios, and antique shops.*

A footbridge reaches into a vast marsh (left) toward Barnstable Harbor on Cape Cod Bay. A mecca for bird watchers, the boardwalk was funded, curiously, by the U.S. Department of Housing and Urban Development and by beach fees collected by residents. The Cape is not all sublime, however. It has an abundance of prosaic amenities as well—pubs, ice cream parlors, bagel shops, taffy stores, and beach shops like this $2 T-shirt Outlet on U.S. Highway 6 in South Wellfleet (above). The Cape's sea air, combined with excursions to Sandwich's Heritage Plantation, Woods Hole's National Marine Fisheries Aquarium—the nation's oldest aquarium—Chatham's lighthouse, or any of a number of whale-watching venues can build up an appetite, easily sated in Cape restaurants of every description and price range.

Hoxie House (above), overlooking Shawme Pond and a waterwheel gristmill in Sandwich—the oldest of Cape Cod's fifteen towns—is a classic shingle saltbox. It has been restored to the period of its construction in 1675. Furnished by the Boston Museum of Fine Arts, it displays a collection of antique textile looms. Cape Cod seems like an island because the 17.4-mile-long Cape Cod Canal between Buzzards and Cape Cod bays separates it from the "mainland." The canal, first proposed by George Washington, was not completed until 1914. The 1934 Sagamore Bridge (opposite) over the canal connects the Upper Cape with Massachusetts' South Shore. As the easiest route for Boston vacationers, the 616-foot span—one of the nation's longest truss bridges—is a dreaded bottleneck on summer Friday and Sunday afternoons. The similar Bourne Bridge, southward down the canal, is the preferred entryway for visitors from Rhode Island.

Plimoth Plantation (opposite) in Plymouth, Massachusetts, re-creates life at the time America's most famous immigrants, the Pilgrims, came to the New World. The living-history museum presents a 1627 Pilgrim village, a Wampanoag Indian homesite, and—elsewhere in downtown Plymouth —a reproduction of the Pilgrims' ship, Mayflower II. Re-enactors speak among themselves in the language of the early seventeenth century. The 116-foot monument to Myles Standish (left), one of Plymouth Colony's founders, overlooks Plymouth Harbor and Duxbury Bay. What is recognized as a piece of Plymouth Rock (above) marks the Pilgrim landing place in 1620. It is enclosed in a Grant's Tomb– type peristyle in downtown Plymouth.

The "Old House" (above) in Quincy, Massachusetts, was home to two presidents: John and John Quincy Adams. The house was occupied by four generations of Adamses—arguably America's greatest intellectual and political family. Unlike even Mount Vernon in Virginia, it never passed out of family hands, and its furnishings have not had to be sought out or replaced. The house is now a National Park Service site. The common and pond in the Massachusetts South Shore ship-building town Cohasset (right) are quintessential New England. Cohasset had its own Paul Revere story: During the War of 1812, militia captain Peter Lothrup raced on horseback to warn of the arrival of British troops, who were routed by the twelve hundred men who responded to his alarm.

The USS Constitution *(above)* berths in Charlestown Harbor by Boston. Still a commissioned U.S. Navy ship, "Old Ironsides" sometimes sallies forth on special occasions, firing its cannons. On Beaver II *(right)*, a replica of the ship on which colonists staged the famous "Boston Tea Party," visitors watch a re-creation and get a cup of tea. The Bunker Hill Monument *(opposite)* in Charlestown tells the story of the epic Revolutionary War battle and offers a spectacular view of metropolitan Boston. On Massachusetts' North Shore, Marblehead Harbor *(overleaf)* offers a lovely view of Abbot municipal hall where the original Yankee Doodle— or correctly Spirit of '76—painting hangs.

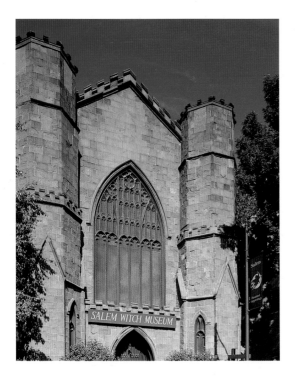

The Witch Museum (above) in Salem, Massachusetts, is quartered in an imposing 1692 Romanesque-style building. It was in the 1690s that the town experienced a reign of terror and hysteria directed at purported witches, some of whom were hanged or pressed to death with heavy stones. Since then, the Salem Witch Trials have been a lamentable yardstick against which due process is measured. The museum features an exhibit entitled, "Do you believe in witches?" Not far away, the dark House of Seven Gables (right) in Salem was the inspiration behind Nathaniel Hawthorne's novel of the same name. Hawthorne often visited his cousin there. The house opened to tours in 1910.

The Paper House
(left) is a curious
New England attrac-
tion in Pigeon Cove,
Massachusetts, north
of Boston. As a hobby
and to experiment
with the use of news-
papers as insulation,
mechanical engineer
Ellis F. Stenman began
building the house out
of newspapers and
magazines in 1922.
Stenman read three
newspapers a day and
collected others from
neighbors. The house
has a wooden frame,
roof, and floor. Its
outer walls, protected
with coats of varnish,
are made from news-
print 215 sheets thick.
The 1923 Gloucester
Fisherman (above) is
that nautical town's
famous symbol, a
memorial to mariners
lost at sea. Commis-
sioned in 1923, it
commemorated the
town's three-hundredth
anniversary.

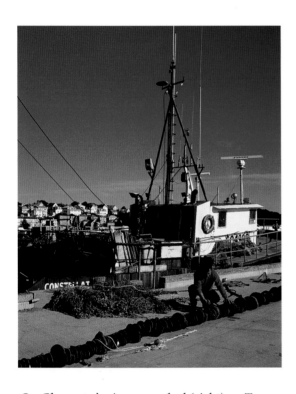

On Gloucester's pier near his trawler, the Constellation, *Nino Guadino* (above) repairs "roll," the part of a commercial fish net that bounces along the sea bottom and keeps the net extended. Gloucester has struggled as North Atlantic marine populations have been overfished. Casino and excursion ships have helped the economy. An unpretentious shed (right) on Tuna Wharf in Rockport, Massachusetts, dubbed "Motif #1" by artists, may be the most famous storage shed in New England. It has been painted by hundreds of artists. Lobster boats and whale-watching cruises depart from this pier, which was built in 1743 and rebuilt on granite blocks in 1811 to dissipate the impact of waves.

Only eighteen miles of New Hampshire border the sea. Part is in charming Portsmouth, home of John Paul Jones's house, other colonial manors, and the original Strawbery Banke settlement, which has been rehabilitated and preserved as a vast living-history museum. In Portsmouth Harbor, Moran Towing Company two- to three-thousand horsepower tugboats (opposite) await assignment to tow ships up the Piscataqua River. South of town, Hampton Beach, home of Guisseppie's Italian Sausage Stand (above), is an old-fashioned beach resort, complete with three-mile boardwalk. On Independence Day weekend especially, the beach is jammed with sun-worshippers. Just across the Maine border, Kittery Point is a delightful fishing village where rowboats are used to get out to moored yachts (overleaf). Kittery is better known, however, as a shoppers' haven. More than 120 outlet stores, selling everything from cologne to waders, line U.S. Highway 1.

The Cape Neddick Light Station (above) in York, Maine, is known as the "Nubble Light," after a nub of rock that juts into the cape. The cast-iron lighthouse, lined in brick, was painted brown when it was completed in 1879. The last keeper left the station in 1987 when the light was automated. But visitors still flock to Sohier Park, which surrounds the old station. Up the road in Wells is the Lighthouse Depot gift shop (opposite) that sells nothing but miniature lighthouses, puzzles, posters, and other lighthouse knickknacks. Because of Maine's treacherous offshore rocks and innumerable inlets, sixty-five lighthouses were built along its shore over 120 years, ending in 1909. Fog is prevalent over the cool waters of the Labrador Current, so most stations were equipped with fog signals, including bells, diaphone horns, steam whistles, and even muzzle-loaded cannons!

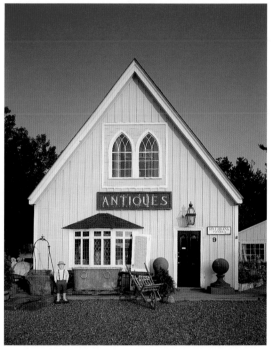

In 1825, shipbuilder George Washington Bourne brought his bride home to the beautiful "Wedding Cake House" (left) that he had built in Kennebunk, Maine. Inspired by a gothic cathedral in Milan, Italy, Bourne added gingerbread details that he fashioned with hand tools. The house was refurbished in 1983–84 by the first owners not of the Bourne family. Still a private residence, it houses an art gallery in the carriage house. Riverbank Antiques (above) is one of eight shops in the Wells Union complex of collectible shops along U.S. Highway 1 north of Wells. The town's shorefront (overleaf) includes an estuarian research reserve on a vast salt marsh.

93

Chris Williams of Gloucester, Massachusetts, sculpted this nine-hundred-pound sheet-metal moose (above) for the Mast Cove Galleries II in Kennebunkport, Maine. A year earlier, he sold a giant metal giraffe there. Ubiquitous inland and upstate, nearsighted moose rarely visit the Maine shore. Human visitors, though—including thousands of Canadians—delight in visiting Old Orchard Beach's elaborate and historic amusement park (right), built in the 1880s. The extensively refurbished array of rides, fun houses, and gustatory pavilions stand on land that was once the first apple orchard in the Western Hemisphere. The park is jammed each June 21 when, as obscure legend has it, the ocean takes on healing powers.

The nation's last active Shaker community can be found near New Gloucester, Maine (left). A century before their numbers dwindled to fewer than ten in the early 1990s, thousands of followers of charismatic founder Ann Lee had flourished in settlements from New England to western Kentucky. Some were early tourist attractions, as travelers came to see the Shakers clap, sing, and dance—with hands cupped to receive God's love or shaking downward to rid themselves of evil. The sect declined, in part, because of its celibate ways. The Wadsworth-Longfellow House (above), part of Portland's three-building "history campus," was built by poet Henry Wadsworth Longfellow's father in 1785.

At the shipbuilding Iron Works (above) in Bath, Maine, a huge industrial crane gets plenty of work. Just down the Kennebec River is a nautical wonderland—the Maine Maritime Museum and Shipyard. The nation's largest wooden ship, the 329-foot Wyoming, was built there in 1909. In fact, the very first ship constructed in the nation—and more than five thousand since—were assembled in these waters. Kennebunkport (right) is a beloved destination for "summer folk" from throughout New England as well as prominent Texans— former president George H. Bush and his family. A colorful little excursion railroad (overleaf) adds to Wiscasset's reputation as the "prettiest town in Maine."

Bell buoys (above) are sold, aptly, at the Bell Buoy #2 Gift Shop in New Harbor, Maine. The store also features "pot buoys" decorated with Santa Claus and other faces. New Harbor is the take-off point for Monhegan Island, a popular Victorian settlement and artist colony. Pemaquid Point (right) in the heart of coastal Maine includes an 1827 lighthouse that now features an art gallery and fishermen's museum. The point's rockbound coast and active fishing villages capture the flavor of coastal Maine. "Recreation," reminds a Pemaquid Area Association pamphlet, "is mostly self-made." Here, though, lolling on the rocks above the ocean, recreation can be a leisurely endeavor.

The economy of tiny Friendship Harbor, Maine, revolves around its pier (opposite), stacked high with lobster traps. Lobsterman Mark Johnson (above), who baits and pulls up traps at the rate of 150 or more a day, lives nearby in Thomaston. Lobster bakes abound, several towns stage lobster festivals, and just about every community sports a "pound," a crude shack that serves the crustacean and little else. Maine may be the "Pine Tree State" and the moose its state animal, but it is the chance to eat— and ship home— lobsters that draws thousands of visitors to the state's rocky shore. Booklets instruct visitors in the indelicate art of eating a lobster, and others show the hard-hearted details of steaming—not boiling, please—the creature to succulent, bright-red perfection. None ever mentions, however, how they get those little, heavy rubber bands over a captured lobster's menacing claws.

*This home (top right) in Port Clyde exemplifies a Maine tradition: connecting one's main house, garage, and other outbuildings to ease passage in Maine's fierce winters. Montpelier museum (bottom right) in Thomaston is a reconstruction of Revolutionary War general Henry Knox's home. Later secretary of war in the nation's first cabinet, Knox forced the British to evacuate Boston by engineering the movement of fifty-nine cannons from Fort Ticonderoga to Dorchester Heights. The original, deteriorated house was razed to make way for a railroad in 1871. Peter Beerits's wooden sculptures are sold at Nervous Nellie's Jams and Jellies (opposite) on Deer Isle, home of the famous Haystack Mountain School of Crafts. Children gather clams at low tide on Lincolnville Beach (overleaf) near fashionable Camden—often called "America's Bed & Breakfast Capital."*

Rockport and Rockland are nearby towns, and both are susceptible to coastal Maine's eerie fogs. Rockport Harbor (above) is home port to both commercial lobster boats and an increasing number of pleasure craft. Remnants of the town's famous kiln that burned lime from deposits on shore can still be seen. Rockland's lighthouse tower (opposite) peeks through the mist along its 4,300-foot sea wall—made over twenty years in the late 1800s from seven hundred thousand tons of cut granite boulders. In 1895, seven years before it was built at the end of the breakwater, a brick fog signal building was constructed. The Rockland Breakwater Light was automated in 1964. Historically a blue-collar fishing town, Rockland is only recently discovering the joys of the tourist economy. Rockland, Rockport, and Camden all offer deep-sea fishing trips and windjammer cruises.

In the mid-nine-
teenth century,
hundreds of ships
were built in Belfast,
Maine (left), and sea
captains set off from
this little town for all
corners of the globe.
When shipbuilding
collapsed, Belfast
became an important
poultry center. Lately,
artists and artisans
have discovered the
gritty town's old fac-
tories, loft apart-
ments, and formerly
abandoned stores. In
Castine is the State
of Maine ship

(above), a teaching
vessel for the Maine
Maritime Academy
in town. Several
months a year, the
ship is a floating lab-
oratory, acquainting
potential merchant
sailors with the rigors
of the high seas. Pic-
turesque Bass Head
Light on the southern
reaches of Mount
Desert Island (over-
leaf) near Tremont,
looms above Bass
Harbor. Built in
1858, the lighthouse
projects an eye-
shaped red beam.

Wilbur the Lobster is the visual attraction—and his smaller, tasty cousins the menu feature—at Ruth and Wimpy's (above) on U.S. Route 1 in Hancock. Wilbur earns his keep; each summer weekend, the "pound" sells as much as four hundred pounds of lobster. In the mid-1800s, Bar Harbor (right) on Maine's Mount Desert Island was the gracious retreat of "summer people" to rival Newport. The introduction of the automobile to the island and the establishment of Lafayette (later Acadia) National Park on the heights overlooking Bar Harbor in the early twentieth century quickly produced overcrowding. A devastating fire in 1947 wiped out old hotels and one-third of the town's great homes, but it provided an impetus for an upgrade of existing properties as well.

Not every accommodation in and near Bar Harbor is luxurious. Quarters like Emery's Cottages (above) in Sand Point, near the Hulls Cove entrance to Acadia National Park, offer a simpler alternative. The formation known as the Raven's Nest (opposite) towers above the Schoodic Peninsula in another stretch of the far-flung national park. This is true "Downeast Maine" where the coastline runs more easterly into the North Atlantic than northward toward Canada. Tourists rarely venture as far as Jonesport (overleaf); indeed, many high-quality guides to Maine or the New England Coast simply stop at Bar Harbor as if the remote counties beyond simply did not exist. Jonesport goes about its business as a fishing and lobstering town with few interruptions from visitors. Here, the lobster is cheaper, the accents authentic Downeast, the winters colder, and the sunrises over the Atlantic breathtaking.

Franklin Roosevelt and his parents, as well as other wealthy Americans, summered on the Canadian island of Campobello in a rustic cottage (left) that Franklin, his wife Eleanor, and their children came to adore. After Franklin was stricken with polio on the island in 1921, Campobello became Eleanor's escape from the rigors of public life. The compound is now an international park, uniquely administered and staffed equally by Canadians and Americans. In Lubec, at the entrance to Cobscook Bay across from New Brunswick, stands the candy-striped, brick-clad, cast-iron West Quoddy Head Light (above). A companion East Quoddy Light can be found on Campobello Island.

127

CANADA

MAINE

Grand... Island

Bangor

Mt. Desert Island

Isle au Haut

Penobscot Bay

95

Waterville

⭐ Augusta

Brunswick

South Portland

40

Distance in miles

N

20

0

ATLANTIC OCEAN

Kittery Point

Lewiston Auburn

495

Portland

Saco
Biddeford

Somersworth

Portsmouth

Amesbury

Cape Cod

Cape Cod

6

Berlin

**Wedding Cake House**

Sanford

Rochester

Dover

95

Lawrence

Medford

Weymouth

495

93

NEW HAMPSHIRE

Concord ⭐

Manchester

Derry

Nashua

⭐ Boston

Worcester

95

Brockton

89

91

Lebanon

**House of Seven Gables**

MASSACHUSETTS

**Hammersmith Farm**

93

Lake Champlain

Burlington
South Burlington

⭐ Montpelier

89

VERMONT

Rutland

Keene

91

Springfield

91

90

Falls

Springs